Table of Contents

INTRODUCTION 1

CHAPTER ONE 3

TAKE PHOTOS 3

    IPhone 15 camera basics: 3

    Use iPhone camera tools to set up your shot: 7

    Apply Photographic Styles with your iPhone 15 camera: 12

    Capture some Live Photos with your iPhone 15 camera: 14

    Burst mode on your iPhone 15 camera: 15

    Ready to snap that perfect selfie with your iPhone 15 camera: ... 16

    Capture stunning panoramic photos with your iPhone camera: 19

    Want to capture stunning close-up shots with your iPhone 15 camera: 20

    Take great portraits with your iPhone 15 camera: 22

    Take Night mode photos with your iPhone 15camera: 29

    Apple ProRAW photos with your iPhone 15 camera: 30

CHAPTER TWO 33

ADJUST THE SHUTTER VOLUME/HDR CAMERA SETTINGS ... 33

ON YOUR IPHONE 15 CAMERA 33

Want to adjust the sound of your iPhone camera's shutter:....... 33

About HDR settings on your iPhone:... 34

CHAPTER THREE 37

HOW TO RECORD ON YOUR IPHONE 15................................. 37

Record videos using your iPhone 15 camera:............................ 37

Record spatial videos for Apple Vision Pro with your iPhone 15 camera: 44

Capturing those cinematic moments:.. 48

CHAPTER FOUR 51

SETTINGS 51

IPhone's video recording settings:... 51

Save your camera settings on your iPhone 15: 54

Adjusting advanced camera settings on your iPhone 15: 57

CHAPTER FIVE 61

MAIN CAMERA LENS... 61

Customize the Main camera lens: 61

Let's explore how you can view, share, and print photos on your iPhone 15: 62

Let's explore how you can use Live Text with your iPhone 15 camera: 64

Scanning a QR code with your iPhone camera: 66

CONCLUSION 69

INTRODUCTION

In the world of technology that's always changing, iPhones have been leading the way. They've changed how we see and interact with the world. Each new iPhone brings something new, and the iPhone 15 is no different. One big highlight of this phone is its amazing camera system.

In this book, you're going on a journey to explore what the iPhone 15's camera can do. We'll dive into all its cool features and uncover the secrets behind the stunning photos it takes. From super clear pictures to movie-like videos, you'll see the magic in every shot.

But this isn't just about tech stuff. It's also about being creative. We'll show you how the iPhone 15 lets anyone, whether you're just starting out or a pro, take awesome pictures with lots of detail and style. With expert advice, useful tips, and examples that'll inspire you, you'll learn how to get the most out of this amazing tool. You'll turn ordinary moments into something extraordinary.

Whether you love taking pictures or you're just curious about cool gadgets, "Unlocking the Lens: Exploring the Revolutionary Camera of the iPhone 15" is your ticket to a journey through innovation. Get ready to feel inspired, hooked, and forever amazed by what the iPhone 15's camera can do.

CHAPTER ONE

TAKE PHOTOS

IPhone 15 camera basics:

Let's get into the basics of using your iPhone camera 📷. You can take photos in different ways, like regular photos, videos, panoramas, and more. Here's how you can do it:

Open Camera:

First, let's open the Camera 📷 app. There are a few ways to do this:

- Tap on the Camera 📷 icon on your iPhone's Home Screen.
- Swipe left on your iPhone's Lock Screen.
- Touch and hold the Camera 📷 icon on your Lock Screen.
- Open the Control Center and tap 📷 on the Camera icon there.

Siri: You can even ask Siri to open the Camera app for you.

- If you have the iPhone 15 Pro or iPhone 15 Pro Max, you can set up the Action button to open the Camera app. You can learn how to do this and more in the iPhone's settings.

NOTE;

Now, when you're using the Camera app, you'll notice a green dot in the top-right corner of your screen. This lets you know that the camera is in use, helping you keep your privacy and security in check.

Take a photo:

To take a photo, just open the Camera 📷 app and tap the Shutter button or press either volume button. Easy, right?

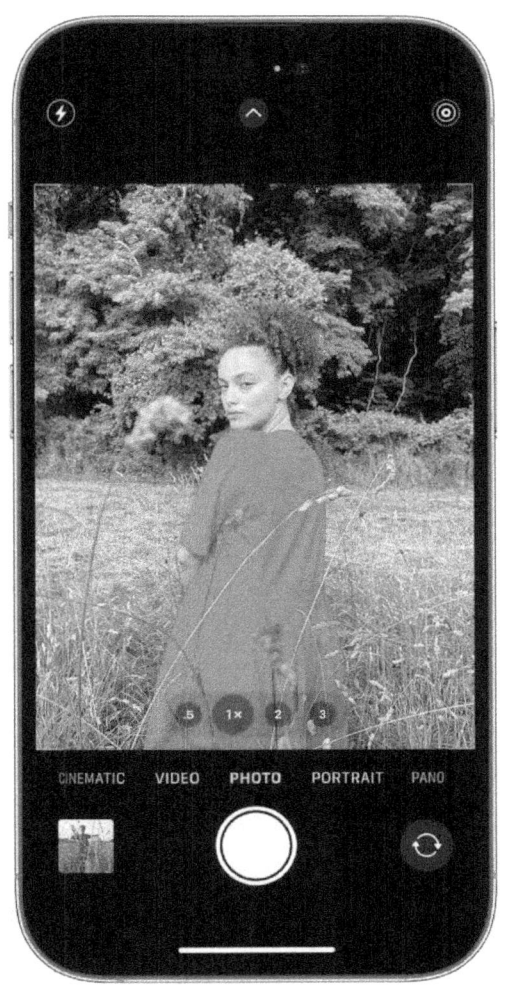

Here's how you can switch between camera modes and use zoom on your iPhone:

When you open your Camera app 📷 , you'll usually start in Photo mode, where you can take regular photos and Live Photos. But if you want to switch things up, just swipe left or right on the camera screen to pick a different mode:

- **Video:** This mode lets you record videos. Check out how to record a video.
- **Time-lapse:** Create cool time-lapse videos that speed up time. Learn how to record a time-lapse video.
- **Slo-mo:** Capture videos with a slow-motion effect. Find out how to record a slow-motion video.
- **Pano:** Take stunning panoramic shots of wide scenes. Discover how to take a panoramic photo.
- **Portrait:** This mode adds a fancy depth-of-field effect to your photos (if your phone supports it). See how to take a portrait in Portrait mode.
- **Cinematic:** Adds depth-of-field to your videos (if your phone supports it). Learn how to record Cinematic videos.
- **Square:** Take photos in a square format.
- **On iPhone 15 and later:** You can tap ⌃, then tap 4:3 to choose between Square, 4:3, or 16:9 aspect ratios.

- To set a mode other than Photo as your default, check out how to save camera settings on iPhone.

About zooming:

- **On all models:** Open Camera 📷 and pinch the screen to zoom in or out.
- **On iPhones with Dual and Triple camera systems:** You can switch between different zoom levels like 0.5x, 1x, 2x, 2.5x, 3x, and 5x (depending on your model). For a more precise zoom, touch and hold the zoom controls, then drag the slider right or left.

Use iPhone camera tools to set up your shot:

Before you snap a picture, you can tweak the focus and exposure settings to get the perfect shot.

The iPhone camera 📷 usually handles focus and exposure automatically, even balancing exposure across multiple faces with face detection. But if you want to take manual control:

1. Open your Camera app.

2. Tap the screen to reveal the automatic focus area and exposure setting.

3. Move the focus area by tapping where you want it.

4. Adjust the exposure by ☀ dragging up or down next to the focus area.

By following these steps, you can fine-tune your photos and capture exactly what you want.

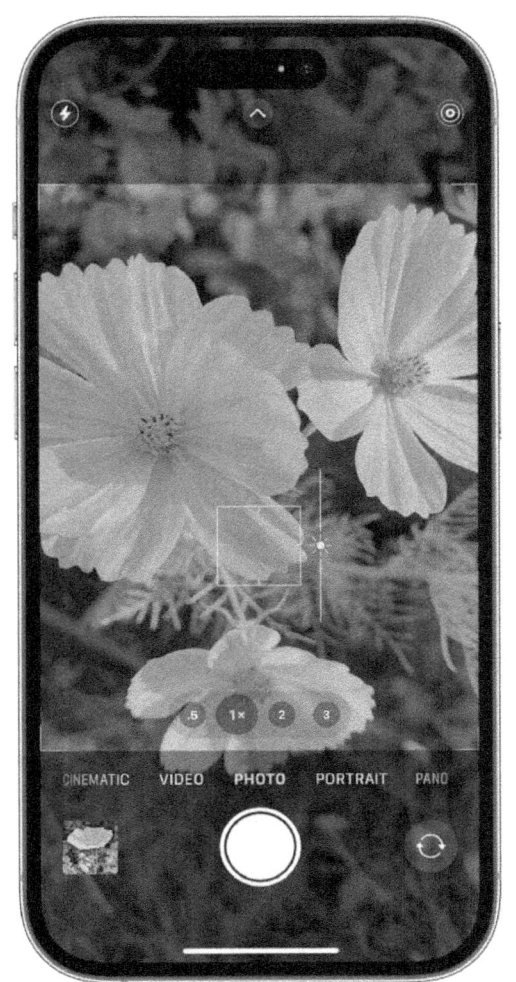

Tips:

"Want to keep your camera settings just right for your next shots?

Easy! Just touch and hold the focus area until you see 'AE/AF Lock.'

Then, tap the screen to unlock.

If you've got an iPhone 15 or newer, you've got even more control. Tap ⌃, tap ⊕ again, and slide the bar to adjust your exposure exactly how you want it. Your exposure stays put until you open the Camera next time. And if you want to keep your exposure settings, go to Settings ⚙ > Camera > Preserve Settings, and switch on 'Exposure Adjustment.'

Turn the flash on or off:

Need to turn the flash on or off? Your iPhone usually does it automatically, but you can take charge. Before snapping a pic, here's what you do:"

Here's how you can make your iPhone camera work just the way you want it to:

- Tap to ⚡ turn automatic flash on or off.

- Tap ⌃, then tap ⚡ below the frame to choose Auto, On, or Off.

Add a Filter to Your Photo:

Want to add some color effects to your photos? Here's how:

1. Open Camera and choose Photo or Portrait mode.
2. Tap ⌃, then tap ⊛.
3. Swipe left or right to preview filters; tap one to use it.
4. Snap your photo with the filter you picked.

Use the Timer:

Need time to get into your shot? Set a timer:

1. Open Camera, then tap ⌃.
2. Tap ⏲, then choose 3s or 10s.
3. Hit the Shutter button to start the timer.

Straighten Your Shot with a Grid and Level:

To keep your shots straight and composed:

Go to Settings ⚙ > Camera.

Turn on Grid and Level. After snapping a photo, you can use editing tools in the Photos app to tweak perspective and alignment. Check out "Straighten and Adjust Perspective."

Apply Photographic Styles with your iPhone 15 camera:

"Did you know you can make your photos look even better with Photographic Styles? If you have a supported model, Camera 📷 lets you choose from preset styles like Rich Contrast, Vibrant, Warm, or Cool. Plus, you can tweak them to match your taste by adjusting the tone and warmth values. Every time you snap a pic in Photo mode, your chosen style will be applied. And the best part? You can switch up or fine-tune your Photographic Styles right there in Camera.

Choose a Photographic Style:

By default, your iPhone camera is set to Standard, which gives you a balanced, true-to-life look. But if you want to spice things up, here's what you can do:"

1. Open up your Camera app 📷, then tap ⌃ here.

2. Now, tap ⌘ this icon, and swipe left to preview different styles:

- Rich Contrast: For darker shadows, richer colors, and stronger contrast, giving your photos a dramatic flair.
- Vibrant: Get ready for wonderfully bright and vivid colors, creating a brilliant yet natural look.
- Warm: Enjoy golden undertones for a warmer vibe.
- Cool: Blue undertones for a cooler feel.

To make a style your own, tap on the Tone and Warmth controls below the frame. Then, slide the slider left or right to adjust the value. If you need to start fresh, just tap ↺ here to reset the values.

3. Tap ⌘ here to apply your chosen Photographic Style.

If you want to tweak or change the style you've chosen, simply tap ⌘ here at the top of the screen. And if you're ready to go back to basics, just select 'Standard' from the style choices.

You can also change Photographic Styles in Settings: go to Settings ⚙ > Camera > Photographic Styles.

Capture some Live Photos with your iPhone 15 camera:

Using your 📷 Camera app, you can easily snap Live Photos, which capture moments just before and after you take the picture, along with the sound. It's like having a mini video clip with your photo!

1. Open up your Camera app.
2. Make sure you're in Photo mode, and double-check that Live Photo is turned on.

When Live Photo is active, you'll see the Live Photo button ◎ at the top of your screen. If there's a slash through it, that means it's turned off. Just tap the button to toggle Live Photo on or off.

3. Now, simply tap the Shutter button to snap your Live Photo.

4. To see your Live Photo in action, tap on the thumbnail at the bottom of your screen. Hold your finger on the screen to watch it play, and release to pause.

Burst mode on your iPhone 15 camera:

Burst mode is your go-to when you're chasing after a moving subject or aiming to snap a series of quick-fire shots. It's perfect for ensuring you have plenty of options to choose from. And guess what? You can use Burst mode with both your rear and front-facing cameras .

Here's how to get started:

1. Open up your Camera app on your iPhone.
2. Swipe the Shutter button to the left and hold it there.
3. Keep your finger on the button to keep snapping those burst shots. Lift your finger when you're done.
4. Now, to pick out your favorite shots from the burst, tap on the Burst thumbnail. You'll see gray dots below the thumbnails, suggesting which photos are worth keeping.

5. Tap on the circle in the lower-right corner of each photo you want to save individually, then hit Done.

And if you've changed your mind and want to scrap the entire burst, no worries! Just tap the thumbnail, then hit the trash 🗑 icon.

Tip for you:

- You can also use the volume up button to take Burst shots. Just head to Settings ⚙ > Camera, and switch on 'Use Volume Up for Burst'.

Ready to snap that perfect selfie with your iPhone 15 camera:

You can take selfies using your Camera 📷 app in Photo mode, Portrait mode, or even Video mode.

Here's how:

1. Open up your Camera app 📷 on your iPhone.

2. Tap 🔄 here to switch to the front-facing camera.

3. Hold your iPhone in front of you, ready to strike your best pose.

Quick Tip: Want to widen your shot? Just tap the arrows inside the frame to expand the field of view.

4. When you're all set, go ahead and tap the Shutter button or press either volume button to snap the shot or start recording.

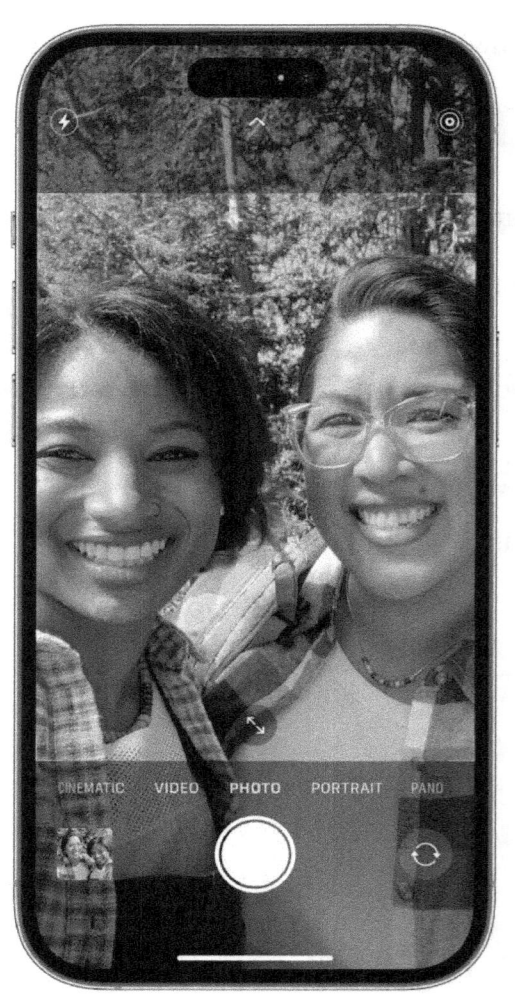

To ensure your selfie is captured exactly as you see it in the front-facing camera frame, without any mirroring, head over to Settings > Camera, and flip the switch to 'Mirror Front Camera'.

Capture stunning panoramic photos with your iPhone camera:

1. Open up your Camera 📷 app on your iPhone.
2. Select the Pano mode from the options available.
3. When you're ready, tap the Shutter button to start capturing your panoramic view.
4. Slowly move your iPhone in the direction of the arrow you see on your screen. Try to keep it aligned with the center line for the best results.
5. Once you're done, tap the Shutter button again to finish capturing your panoramic masterpiece.

Remember, if you want to pan in the opposite direction, just tap the arrow on your screen. And if you prefer to capture a vertical panorama, simply rotate your iPhone to landscape orientation. You can even change the direction of your vertical pan if you need to!

Want to capture stunning close-up shots with your iPhone 15 camera:

You can take amazing macro photos and videos with ease! Here's how:

Taking a Macro Photo or Video:

1. Open up your Camera app 📷 on your iPhone and choose either Photo or Video mode.
2. Get up close to your subject, as close as 2 centimeters. Your iPhone will automatically switch to the Ultra Wide camera for that perfect macro shot.
3. Tap the Shutter button to snap a photo or the Record button to start and stop recording your macro video.

Capturing Macro Slow-Motion or Time-Lapse Videos:

1. Open your Camera 📷 app again, but this time select Slo-mo or Time-lapse mode.

2. Switch to the Ultra Wide camera by tapping .5x, then move in close to your subject.

3. Press the Record button to begin and end your macro slow-motion or time-lapse recording.

Controlling Automatic Macro Switching:

If you prefer to have more control over when your camera switches to macro mode, follow these steps:

1. Open your Camera app, and as you approach a subject within macro distance, you'll see a prompt on your screen.

2. Tap 🌷 the prompt to turn off automatic macro switching. If you want it back on, just tap it again.

Tip: If your photo or video seems blurry, try backing up a bit or tapping .5x to switch to the Ultra Wide camera.

3. Adjusting Macro Control Settings 🌷

To customize how your iPhone handles macro shots:

Go to Settings ⚙ > Camera and adjust the Macro Control settings to your liking.

If you want these settings to stick between camera sessions, head to Settings ⚙ > Camera > Preserve Settings and toggle on Macro Control.

Now you're all set to capture incredible close-up moments with your iPhone camera!

Take great portraits with your iPhone 15 camera:

When your iPhone model supports Portrait mode, you can create portraits with a cool depth-of-field effect. This keeps your subject—whether it's people, pets, or objects—crisp while blurring the background for a stunning look. Plus, you can tweak different lighting effects to make your portraits even better.

To take a portrait in Portrait mode, follow these steps:

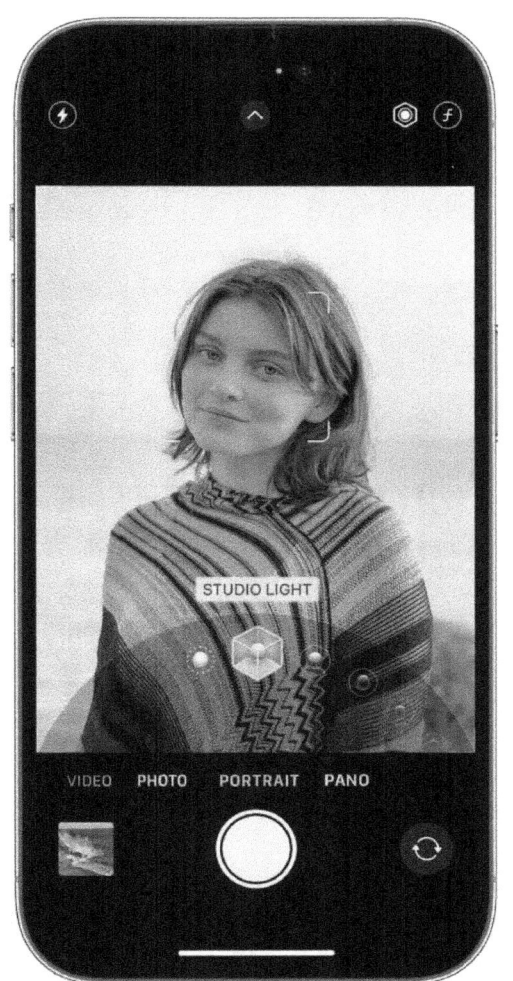

1. Open your Camera app 📷 and select Portrait mode.

2. If needed, follow the on-screen tips to frame your subject in the yellow portrait box.

"When you're using supported models, just tap once, twice, or three times to switch between different zoom options.

If you're using an iPhone 15, you can simply pinch the screen to zoom in and out.

3. Now, let's talk about choosing a lighting effect.

- **Natural Light:** Your face will stand out sharply against a blurred background.
- **Studio Light:** Your face will be well-lit, giving the whole photo a clean look.
- **Contour Light:** This will create dramatic shadows and highlights on your face.
- **Stage Light:** Your face will be spotlighted against a deep black background.
- **Stage Light Mono:** Similar to Stage Light, but your photo will be in classic black and white.
- **High-Key Light Mono:** This creates a grayscale image with your subject on a white background."

4. When you're ready to capture the perfect moment, just tap the Shutter button.

After you've taken a photo in Portrait mode, you have the power to adjust it to your liking. Simply open the photo in the Photos app, tap Edit, and then tap Portrait to toggle the effect on or off.

NOTE;

- If you're using supported models, Night mode kicks in automatically when you're capturing a portrait in low-light situations with the wide (1x) lens. For more details on Night mode, check out the section on taking Night mode photos.
- Photographic Styles are automatically applied to portraits taken in Portrait mode.
- If you're using an iPhone 15, keep in mind that Stage Light, Stage Light Mono, and High-Key Light Mono are exclusive to the front camera."

This version maintains readability while giving the feeling that the book is speaking directly to you.

Adjust Depth Control in Portrait mode:

Use the Depth Control slider to adjust the level of background blur in your portraits.

1. Open Camera 📷, select Portrait mode, then frame your subject.

2. Tap *f* in the top-right corner of the screen.

The Depth Control slider appears below the frame.

3. Drag the slider to the right or left to adjust the effect.

4. Tap the Shutter button to take the shot.

After you capture a portrait, you can use the Depth Control slider in the Photos app to further adjust the background blur effect.

Adjust Portrait Lighting in Portrait mode:

You can virtually adjust the position and intensity of the Portrait Lighting to sharpen eyes or brighten and smooth facial features.

1. Open Camera, select Portrait mode, then drag to choose a lighting effect.

2. Tap at the top of the screen.

The Portrait Lighting slider appears below the frame.

3. Drag the slider to the right or left to adjust the effect.

4. Tap the Shutter button to take the shot.

After you capture a portrait, you can edit the Portrait Lighting levels in the Photos app.

Take a portrait in Photo mode:

On iPhone 15 models, you can apply the portrait effect and blur the background on photos taken in Photo mode.

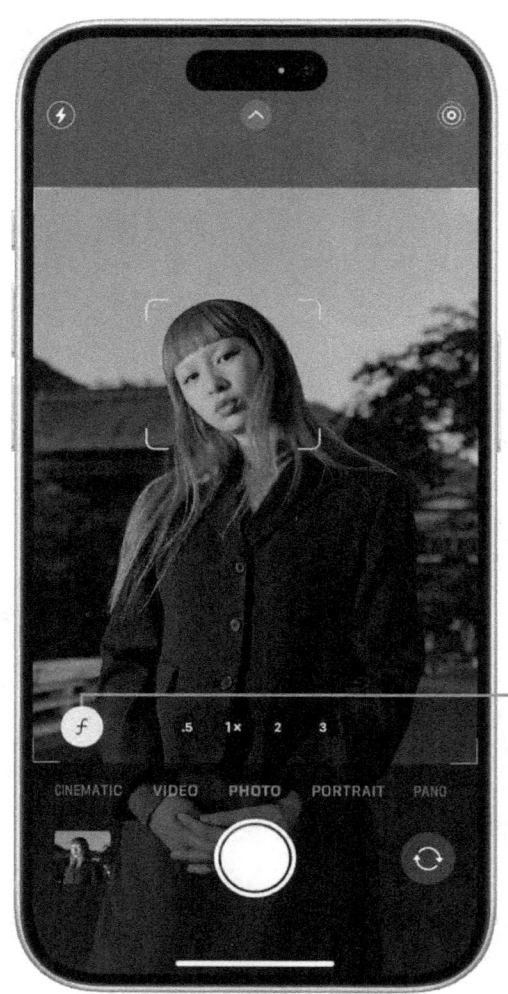

Tap to turn portrait effects on and off in Photo mode.

1. Open Camera .

If your iPhone detects a person, dog, or cat, automatically appears at the bottom of the view finder.

Note: Your iPhone captures depth information when ƒ appears while taking photos in Photo mode, so if you decide not to apply the portrait effect when you take the shot, you can apply it later in the Photos app .

2. If ƒ doesn't appear, tap a subject in the view finder to focus on it and ƒ will appear. If you want to change the focus point of the portrait, tap a different subject in the view finder.

3. Tap ƒ, then tap the Shutter button to take the photo with the portrait effect.

Note: Photographic Styles are applied to portraits that you take in Photo mode.

Take Night mode photos with your iPhone 15camera:

On supported models, Camera can use Night mode to capture more detail and brighten your shots in low-light situations. The length of the exposure in Night mode is determined automatically, but you can experiment with the manual controls.

Tip: Use a tripod for even more detailed Night mode photos.

Night mode is available on the following iPhone models and cameras:

- iPhone 15 Pro, iPhone 15 Pro Max.
- iPhone 15 models.

Apple ProRAW photos with your iPhone 15 camera:

If your iPhone supports it, you've got the power to take stunning photos in Apple ProRAW format. This special format combines the benefits of a standard RAW file with the magic of iPhone image processing, giving you more flexibility to tweak things like exposure, color, and white balance later on.

Here's how to get set up with Apple ProRAW:

First off, head to your Settings ⚙, then tap on Camera, and then Formats. From there, flip the switch to turn on Apple ProRAW or

ProRAW & Resolution Control, depending on your iPhone model. Just a heads up, though: since Apple ProRAW captures more data, your photo files might end up a bit larger.

Now, let's snap a photo using Apple ProRAW:

1. Open up your Camera app, and you'll see a little icon—either a R̶A̶W̶ or a RAW MAX, depending on your iPhone model.
2. Tap on that to turn on ProRAW. Then, take your shot as usual.

While you're shooting, you can easily switch RAW on or R̶A̶W̶ by tapping that same icon.

If you want to keep using ProRAW for all your shots, head back to Settings ⚙, then Camera, and Preserve Settings. Toggle on Apple ProRAW or ProRAW & Resolution Control to make sure your choice sticks.

Change the default resolution and format:

For iPhone 15 Pro and iPhone 15 Pro Max users, you've got options.

1. Head back to Settings ⚙, then Camera, and Formats.

1. Turn on ProRAW & Resolution Control.

2. Tap on Pro Default, Pick your preferred resolution and format—either HEIF Max, ProRAW 12 MP, ProRAW Max.

Just a quick note: if you've set your Camera Capture to Most Compatible, your photos will default to JPEG Max instead of HEIF Max.

CHAPTER TWO

ADJUST THE SHUTTER VOLUME/HDR CAMERA SETTINGS ON YOUR IPHONE 15 CAMERA

Want to adjust the sound of your iPhone camera's shutter:

Easy! You can make it louder or mute it altogether using the Ring/Silent switch on the side of your iPhone .

To change the shutter sound volume in Photo mode:

1. Open the Camera app and switch to Photo mode.
2. Swipe up or down in Control Center to adjust the volume .
3. Swipe back down to return to Camera.

Note: Live Photos won't make a shutter sound (except in certain countries and regions).

To mute the shutter sound completely:

Just flip the Ring/Silent switch on the side of your iPhone to Silent mode. You'll see it turn orange. To bring back the sound, just flip it back.

For iPhone 15 Pro and iPhone 15 Pro Max users:

Instead of a Ring/Silent switch, you have an Action button. This button can also toggle Silent mode, along with other functions.

Note: In some places, you might not be able to mute the shutter sound.

About HDR settings on your iPhone:

HDR (high dynamic range) in Camera 📷 helps you capture amazing shots, especially in high-contrast scenes. Your iPhone takes a bunch of quick shots at different exposures and blends them for better detail in highlights and shadows.

By default, your iPhone automatically switches to HDR mode when it's most helpful. And if you've got an iPhone 15 model, it even records videos in HDR for lifelike colors and contrast.

If you want to turn off automatic HDR:

"Your iPhone is pretty smart—it automatically switches to HDR when it'll make your photos look their best. But guess what? You can also take the reins and control HDR yourself on some models.

If you've got an iPhone 15, here's how you do it:

- Head to Settings ⚙ > Camera.
- Turn off Smart HDR.

Now, when you're in the camera app, just tap on HDR to toggle it on or off.

Want to tweak HDR for videos:

On iPhone 15 models, your phone records videos in Dolby Vision HDR, making colors and contrast pop. But if you prefer to turn off HDR for videos:

- Go to Settings ⚙ > Camera > Record Video.

- Switch off HDR Video.

CHAPTER THREE

HOW TO RECORD ON YOUR IPHONE 15

Record videos using your iPhone 15 camera:

To record videos, you can use your iPhone's Camera app. You can take different types of videos like Cinematic, slow-motion, and time-lapse videos.

Record a video:

1. Open your Camera app and select the Video mode.
2. Tap the Record button or press either volume button to start recording.

- While recording, you can take a still photo by pressing the white Shutter button.
- Zoom in and out by pinching the screen, or adjust the zoom more precisely by touching and holding 1x and then dragging the slider (if your model supports it).

3. Tap the Record button or press either volume button again to stop recording.

Note: Remember, when you're using the Camera, a green dot appears at the top of the screen for your security.

If you want to record in HD or 4K resolution:

1. Go to Settings ⚙ > Camera > Record Video.
2. Choose from the list of video formats and frame rates your iPhone supports.

Use Action mode:

On iPhone 15 models, there's an Action mode that improves stabilization while recording. You can turn it on and off by tapping the icons at the top 🏃 of the screen.

38

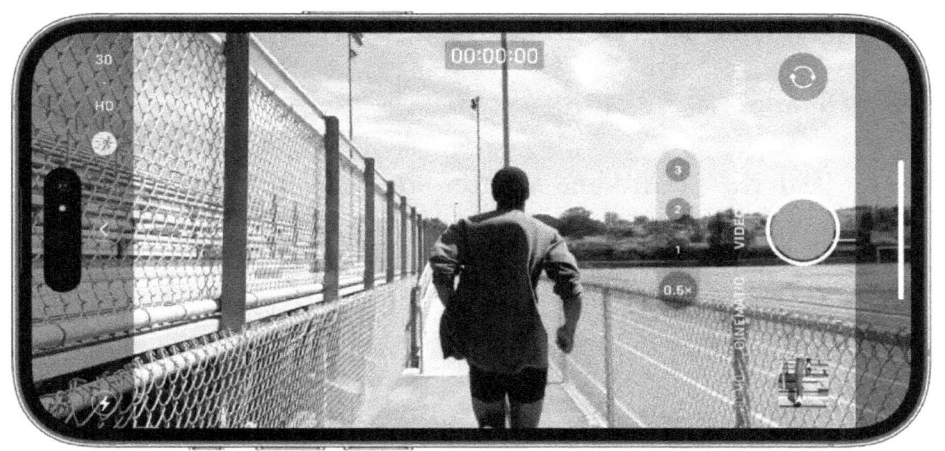

NOTE:

"Hey there! Just a heads-up: Action mode shines brightest in well-lit environments. But if you're itching to use it in lower light situations, no worries! You can tweak some settings.

Here's what you do:

A QuickTake video is like magic—you capture it while in Photo mode. And get this: while you're recording, you can even snap still photos.

Here's your step-by-step guide:

1. Open up Camera. Press and hold the Shutter button to kick off your QuickTake video.

2. Slide that same button to the right and release it to lock it for hands-free recording.

- Both the Record and Shutter buttons will be right below the frame. Tap the Shutter button to snag a still shot while you're still rolling.
- Need to zoom in? Swipe up on the screen. And if you're hands-free, just pinch out to zoom.

3. When you're all done, tap the Record button to wrap it up.

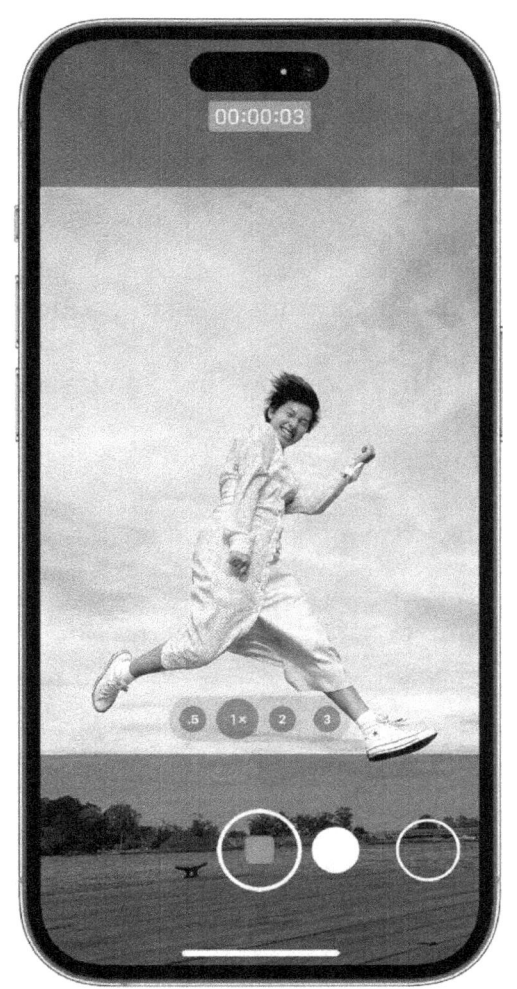

"**QuickTip:**

Want to start recording a QuickTake video in Photo mode? Easy peasy! Just press and hold either the volume up or volume down button.

And when you're done, just tap on the thumbnail to check out your QuickTake video in the Photos app.

Slow-motion videos:

When you're recording in Slo-mo mode, your video records just like usual, but you'll get that cool slow-motion effect when you play it back. Plus, you can even tweak your video so that the slow-motion kicks in and ends exactly when you want it to."

1. Open up Camera and pick Slo-mo mode.

On iPhone 15 models, you can even switch to Slo-mo mode with the front camera by tapping here.

2. Once you're set up, hit that Record button or just press one of the volume buttons to start rolling.

You can snap a still photo while recording by tapping the Shutter button.

3. When you're all done, tap the Record button again or hit a volume button to stop recording. Easy, right?

If you want part of your video to be in slow motion and the rest at regular speed, no problem! Just tap on the video thumbnail, then hit Edit. Slide those bars below the frame to choose which part you want to slow down.

And hey, depending on your iPhone model, you can tweak the slow-motion settings. Just head to Settings ⚙ > Camera > Record Slo-mo.

Quick tip: you can adjust the video resolution and frame rate on the fly while you're recording.

Switch gears and talk time-lapse:

1. Open up Camera and select Time-lapse mode.
2. Get your iPhone set up to capture whatever scene you want to watch unfold.
3. Hit that Record button to start, and hit it again when you're ready to wrap things up.

Tips: If you're using an iPhone 15 or newer, using a tripod can really enhance your time-lapse videos, especially in low-light situations.

Record spatial videos for Apple Vision Pro with your iPhone 15 camera:

"Ready to bring your memories to life in three dimensions? Let's get started on recording spatial videos with your iPhone camera

Note: This feature is available on iPhone 15 Pro and iPhone 15 Pro Max models with iOS 17.2 or later.

Recording a spatial video:

1. Open up your 📷 Camera app on your iPhone 15 Pro or iPhone 15 Pro Max.
2. Switch to Video mode and make sure your iPhone is turned sideways for landscape orientation.
3. Tap ∞ here, then hit that Record button or press either volume button to begin recording. For the best results, remember to:

- Keep your iPhone steady and level.
- Position your subjects 3 to 8 feet away from the camera.

- Use bright and even lighting.

4. When you're finished, tap the Record button again or press either volume button to stop recording.

5. Tap 👓 here to turn off spatial video recording.

Once you've recorded your spatial video, get ready to experience those moments in three dimensions on your Apple Vision Pro. And the best part? You can also watch these videos in two dimensions and share them just like regular videos on your other Apple devices. They'll sync across all your devices where you're signed in with the same Apple ID and have iCloud Photos turned on.

Note: Spatial videos recorded on iPhone 15 Pro and iPhone 15 Pro Max are in 1080p resolution at 30 frames per second in SDR. Just remember, one minute of spatial video takes up around 130 MB, while one minute of regular 1080p 30 fps video is about 65 MB.

Recording ProRes videos with your iPhone camera;

"Exciting news! If you've got a supported model, you can now use your 📷 Camera app to record and tweak videos in ProRes format.

What's ProRes, you ask? Well, it's all about giving you richer colors and less compression in your videos.

But here's the lowdown: ProRes isn't available in Cinematic, Time-lapse, or Slo-Mo mode. And keep in mind, ProRes videos tend to take up more space on your device.

Ready to dive in and set up ProRes:

Head over to Settings ⚙ > Camera > Formats, then switch on Apple ProRes.

Start recording with ProRes:

1. Open up your Camera app, select Video mode, and tap ProRes HDR here to enable ProRes.

2. Hit that Record button or press one of the volume buttons to kick off your recording.

And hey, while you're recording with the rear camera, here are some nifty tricks:

- Pinch to zoom in or out.

- Tap to switch between different lenses.

- Or touch and hold the lens chooser to get more precise zoom control.

3. When you're all done, tap the Record button again or hit a volume button to wrap it up.

4. And if you want to turn off ProRes, just tap ProRes here.

ProRes gives you the option to record up to 4K at 30 fps. But if you've got an iPhone 15 Pro or iPhone 15 Pro Max hooked up to the right external storage, you can even push it to 4K at 60 fps.

Quick note: If you're using a 128 GB iPhone model, you'll be limited to recording at 1080p at 30 fps, except for the iPhone 15 Pro 128 GB models, which can handle 4K up to 60 fps with the right external storage. For more info, check out the Apple Support article About Apple ProRes on iPhone.

Choose color encoding options for your ProRes recordings:

On iPhone 15 Pro and iPhone 15 Pro Max, you can even choose between HDR, SDR, or Log color encoding for your ProRes recordings.

1. First things first, head over to Settings ⚙ > Camera > Formats, and switch on Apple ProRes.
2. Now, tap on ProRes Encoding, and choose between HDR, SDR, or Log for your video encoding.

Capturing those cinematic moments:

Cinematic mode adds a beautiful depth-of-field effect to your videos, keeping your subject sharp while blurring the background for that cinematic look.

Here's how you do it:

1. Open up your Camera app and select Cinematic mode.

You can tap '3' next to '1x' to zoom in before you start recording.

On iPhone 15 models, you can simply pinch the screen to zoom in or out.

To tweak the depth-of-field effect, tap ⓕ here and slide the slider left or right before you hit that Record button.

2. Once you're all set, go ahead and hit the Record button or press either volume button to start recording.
3. Keep an eye on the screen:
- A yellow frame means the person is in focus.
- A gray frame indicates that a person is detected but not in focus. Tap on the gray box to change the focus, and tap again to lock it.
- If there's no person in the video, just tap anywhere on the screen to set the focus point.
- To lock the focus at a specific distance, simply touch and hold the screen.
- When you're done capturing your cinematic masterpiece, tap the Record button or press either volume button to stop recording.

And here's a handy tip for iPhone 15 users: You can use the quick toggles at the top of the screen to easily adjust the video resolution and frame rate while recording.

Once you've recorded your video in Cinematic mode, you can always remove or change the cinematic effect later. Happy filming!"

CHAPTER FOUR

SETTINGS

IPhone's video recording settings:

By default, the Camera app 📷 records videos at 30 frames per second (fps). However, depending on which iPhone model you have, you can opt for different frame rates and video resolutions. Keep in mind that selecting faster frame rates and higher resolutions will result in larger video files.

To make these adjustments, you can use quick toggles directly on the camera screen:

When you're in Video mode, you'll see quick toggles at the top of the screen that allow you to change the video resolution and frame rates available on your iPhone.

Simply tap on the quick toggles in the top-right corner to switch between HD or 4K recording and 24, 25, 30, or 60 fps, depending on your iPhone model.

If you have an iPhone 15, you'll find similar quick toggles in Cinematic mode to switch between HD or 4K and 24, 25, or 30 fps.

Adjusting Auto FPS Settings:

Your iPhone can automatically adjust the frame rate to 24 fps in low-light situations to enhance video quality.

- To set this up, go to Settings ⚙ > Camera > Record Video, and depending on your iPhone model, you can either enable Auto FPS for 30-fps video or apply it to both 30- and 60-fps video.
- You can also turn on Auto Low Light FPS.

Turning Stereo Recording On and Off:

To achieve stereo sound, your iPhone uses multiple microphones.

If you prefer to turn off stereo recording, simply navigate to Settings ⚙ > Camera, then toggle off Record Stereo Sound.

Turning HDR Video On and Off:

Some iPhone models support recording videos in HDR, which offers enhanced dynamic range.

To toggle HDR recording, go to Settings > Camera > Record Video, then switch HDR Video on or off.

Turning Lock Camera On and Off:

On iPhone 15 models, the Lock Camera feature prevents automatic camera switching during video recording.

To enable Lock Camera, go to Settings > Camera > Record Video, then toggle Lock Camera on.

Turning Enhanced Stabilization On and Off:

Enhanced Stabilization, available on iPhone 15 models, slightly zooms in to provide better stabilization while recording videos.

To disable Enhanced Stabilization, go to Settings > Camera > Record Video, then toggle Enhanced Stabilization off.

Turning Lock White Balance On and Off:

You can lock the white balance when recording videos to ensure accurate color capture based on lighting conditions.

To turn on Lock White Balance, go to Settings > Camera > Record Video, then toggle Lock White Balance on.

With these settings, you can customize your iPhone's video recording experience to suit your preferences.

Save your camera settings on your iPhone 15:

It can be frustrating when you open the Camera app and find that your preferred settings have been reset. Thankfully, you can save your last-used camera mode, filter, lighting, depth, and Live Photo settings so they remain unchanged the next time you open the app.

Here's how you can do it:

1. Go to Settings > Camera > Preserve Settings.
2. Turn on any of the following options:

Camera Mode: This saves the last camera mode you used, whether it's Video, Pano, or another mode.

See Switch between camera modes.

- **Creative Controls:** Preserve the last settings you used for filters, lighting options, or depth control.
- **Macro Control:** This preserves the Auto Macro setting instead of automatically switching to the Ultra Wide camera for macro photos and videos (available on iPhone 15 Pro and iPhone 15 Pro Max).

See Control automatic macro switching.

- **Exposure Adjustment:** Save the exposure control setting (available on iPhone 15 and later).

See Adjust the camera's focus and exposure.

- **Night Mode:** This saves the Night mode setting instead of resetting to Auto (available on iPhone 15 models).

See Take Night mode photos with your iPhone camera.

- **Portrait Zoom:** Preserve the Portrait mode zoom instead of resetting to the default lens (available on iPhone 15 Pro and iPhone 15 Pro Max).

See Take portraits with your iPhone camera.

- **Action Mode:** Keep the Action Mode setting turned on instead of resetting to off (available on iPhone models released later).

- **Apple ProRAW:** Save the Apple ProRAW setting (available on iPhone 15 Pro and iPhone 15 Pro Max).

See Take Apple ProRAW photos with your iPhone camera.

- **Apple ProRes:** Preserve the Apple ProRes setting (available on iPhone 15 Pro and iPhone 15 Pro Max).

See Record ProRes videos with your iPhone camera.

- **Live Photo:** Save the Live Photo setting.

With these settings saved, you can enjoy a more consistent and personalized camera experience on your iPhone.

Now, let's explore how you can change advanced camera settings, starting with adjusting the Main camera resolution.

Adjusting advanced camera settings on your iPhone 15:

Your iPhone's Camera app offers advanced features that enable you to snap photos more efficiently, apply customized enhancements to your pictures, and even preview content beyond the camera frame.

Changing the Main Camera Resolution:

On iPhone 15 models, the default resolution for the Main camera is set to 24 MP. However, you have the option to switch between 12 MP, 24 MP, and 48 MP.

Go to Settings > Camera > Formats > Photo Mode, then select either 12 MP or 24 MP.

For capturing images at 48 MP, navigate to Settings > Camera > Formats, then enable Resolution Control or ProRAW & Resolution Control (depending on your iPhone model).

On iPhone 15 Pro and iPhone 15 Pro Max, after enabling ProRAW & Resolution Control, you can choose the default format by tapping on Pro Default. In the Camera app, toggle the format on or off at the top of the screen. To select a different format, touch and hold the toggle.

Turning View Outside the Frame On and Off:

Certain iPhone models provide a camera preview that displays content beyond the frame, showing you what additional content could be captured using a wider lens. This feature, called View Outside the Frame, is enabled by default.

Go to Settings > Camera, then toggle View Outside the Frame off or on.

Adjusting Prioritize Faster Shooting:

The Prioritize Faster Shooting setting enhances the speed at which images are processed, allowing you to capture multiple photos rapidly by tapping the Shutter button. This feature is enabled by default.

Go to Settings > Camera, then toggle Prioritize Faster Shooting off or on.

Turning Lens Correction On and Off:

On supported iPhone models, Lens Correction adjusts photos taken with the front or Ultra Wide camera to achieve more natural-looking results. This feature is enabled by default.

Go to Settings > Camera, then toggle Lens Correction off or on.

Adjusting Scene Detection:

For iPhone 15 models, Scene Detection identifies the subject of your photo and applies a customized look to enhance its qualities. This feature is enabled by default.

Go to Settings > Camera, then toggle Scene Detection off or on.

By adjusting these advanced camera settings, you can tailor your iPhone's photography experience to suit your preferences and needs.

CHAPTER FIVE

MAIN CAMERA LENS

Customize the Main camera lens:

Let's talk about customizing the main camera lens on your iPhone 15 Pro or iPhone 15 Pro Max. By default, the 1x main camera lens is set at 24 mm. However, you have the option to add secondary lenses like 28 mm and 35 mm, and you can also change which lens you want as the default main lens.

Here's how you can customize your camera settings:

1. Open Settings, then go to Camera > Formats > Photo Mode, and tap on 24 MP.

2. In Settings, tap on Camera, then select Main Camera.

3. Scroll down to Additional Lenses, and toggle on the lenses you want to add as additional Main lenses.

4. Below Default Lens, choose the option you prefer to use as the default Main lens.

5. To exit Settings, simply swipe up from the bottom of the screen.

Once you've set your main camera 📷 lens, open the Camera app. Depending on what you've chosen, the default lens for your main camera will be either 1x (24 mm), 1.2x (28 mm), or 1.5x (35 mm). You can tap on the main camera lens to switch between the additional lenses you've selected.

Let's explore how you can view, share, and print photos on your iPhone 15:

All the photos and videos you capture using the Camera 📷 app are stored in the Photos app. When you have iCloud Photos enabled, any new photos and videos you take are automatically backed up and accessible across all your devices that have iCloud Photos set up (with iOS 8.1, iPadOS 13, or later).

NOTE:

If you've enabled Location Services in Settings > Privacy & Security > Location Services, your photos and videos will be tagged with location data. This information can be utilized by apps and photo-sharing websites.

Now, let's talk about viewing your photos:

Let's dive into how you can view, share, and print your photos on your iPhone:

Viewing Your Photos:

1. Open the Camera app, then tap the thumbnail image in the lower-left corner.
2. Swipe left or right to browse through the photos you've taken recently.
3. Tap the screen to reveal or hide the controls.
4. Tap "All Photos" to access all your photos and videos stored in the Photos app.

Sharing and Printing Your Photos:

1. While viewing a photo, tap on ⬆ it.

2. To share your photo, choose an option like AirDrop, Mail, or Messages.

3. To print your photo, swipe up and select "Print" from the list of actions.

Uploading and Syncing Your Photos Across Devices:

You can use iCloud Photos to upload photos and videos from your iPhone to iCloud, making them accessible on other devices where you're signed in with the same Apple ID. iCloud Photos is handy for keeping your photos synced across multiple devices and saving space on your iPhone. To enable iCloud Photos, go to Settings > Photos.

Let's explore how you can use Live Text with your iPhone 15 camera:

Your Camera 📷 app can do more than just capture photos. It can also recognize text within the camera frame, allowing you to copy, share, look up, and translate text effortlessly. Additionally, it offers quick actions like calling phone numbers, visiting websites, and converting currencies based on the text it detects.

Here's how to use Live Text:

1. Open the Camera app and position your iPhone so that the text you want to interact with appears within the camera frame.
2. Once the yellow frame appears around the detected text, tap ⬚ on it. Then, you can:

- **Copy:** Copy the text to paste it into another app like Notes or Messages.
- **Select All:** Choose to select all the text within the frame.
- **Look Up:** Get personalized web suggestions.
- **Translate:** Instantly translate the text into another language.
- **Search the web:** Look up the selected text online.
- **Share:** Share the text via AirDrop, Messages, Mail, or other available options.

NOTE:

- You can also touch and hold the text to select specific parts and perform the actions mentioned above.

- Quick actions at the bottom of the screen allow you to make phone calls, visit websites, send emails, convert currencies, and more.

3. Tap 🔲 on the "X" icon to return to the Camera app.

To disable Live Text on your iPhone camera, go to Settings ⚙ > Camera, then toggle off "Show Detected Text."

Please note: Live Text may not be available in all regions or languages.

Scanning a QR code with your iPhone camera:

Let's talk about how you can use your iPhone camera to scan QR codes:

Using the Camera 📷 app or the Code Scanner feature, you can effortlessly scan Quick Response (QR) codes. These codes can lead you to websites, apps, coupons, tickets, and more, and your camera automatically detects and highlights them.

Here's how to read a QR code using your camera:

1. Open the Camera app on your iPhone and position it so that the QR code is visible on the screen.
2. Once the QR code is detected, a notification will appear on the screen. Tap on it to be directed to the relevant website or app associated with the code.

Alternatively, you can access the Code Scanner from the Control Center:

1. Go to Settings 🛞 > Control Center, then tap on the ⊕ next to Code Scanner to add it to your Control Center.
2. Open the Control Center by swiping down from the top right corner of your screen. Tap on the Code Scanner icon, then position your iPhone so that the QR code is visible.
3. If you need more light to scan the code, you can tap on the flashlight icon to turn it on.

With these simple steps, you can easily scan QR codes using your iPhone camera or the Code Scanner feature from the Control Center.

CONCLUSION

As we wrap up "Unlocking the Lens: Exploring the Revolutionary Camera of the iPhone 15," it's clear that this journey we've shared has been truly transformative. Throughout our exploration, we've peeled back the layers of innovation and creativity found in the iPhone 15's camera, revealing its remarkable ability to capture moments with incredible clarity and depth.

From learning about its technical capabilities to unlocking its artistic potential, you now have the knowledge and inspiration to make the most of this incredible tool. Whether you're just starting out in photography or you're already a seasoned pro, the iPhone 15's camera offers endless possibilities.

But beyond just pixels and lenses, there's a deeper truth: technology has the power to connect us, to inspire us, and to change how we see the world. As you continue your journey with your iPhone 15, carry with you the spirit of exploration, innovation, and creativity that we've shared.

So, as you go forward, let the lens of your iPhone 15 be your companion as you capture the beauty, wonder, and magic of the world around you. Remember, the adventure never truly ends—it's just waiting for your next shot, your next spark of inspiration, and the next chapter in your photographic journey.

www.ingramcontent.com/pod-product-compliance
Lightning Source LLC
Chambersburg PA
CBHW050237230526
45470CB00005B/1999